From Rubber Tree to Tire

From Rubber Tree to Tire

Ali Mitgutsch

 Carolrhoda Books, Inc., Minneapolis

First published in the United States of America 1986 by Carolrhoda Books, Inc.
Original edition © 1980 by Sellier Verlag GmbH, Eching bei München,
West Germany, under the title VOM KAUTSCHUKSAFT ZUM REIFEN.
Revised English text © 1986 by Carolrhoda Books, Inc.
Illustrations © 1980 by Sellier Verlag GmbH.
All rights reserved.

Manufactured in the United States of America

LIBRARY OF CONGRESS CATALOGING-IN-PUBLICATION DATA

Mitgutsch, Ali.
    From rubber tree to tire.

    (A Carolrhoda start to finish book)
    Translation of: Vom Kautschuksaft zum Reifen.
    Summary: Follows the rubber juice (latex) from its
tree to the factory and eventual use as a tire on
various vehicles.

    1. Tires, Rubber—Juvenile literature. 2. Rubber—
Juvenile literature. [1. Tires, Rubber. 2. Rubber]
I. Title. II. Series.

TS1912.M4913   1986   678'.32   86-17170
ISBN 0-87614-297-8 (lib. bdg.)

  1 2 3 4 5 6 7 8 9 10 96 95 94 93 92 91 90 89 88 87 86

From Rubber Tree to Tire

The hot, moist parts of the world
are called the tropics.
Rubber trees grow in the tropics.
In order to get the rubber out of the trees,
people first cut grooves into the bark
with long, sharp knives.
Then they put a spout into each tree
and hang cups under the spouts.
The rubber juice, called **latex,**
runs down the spouts into the cups.

Every day, people with buckets collect the juice from many, many trees.
The juice is white, like milk.

The latex is then poured into larger containers.

Water is added to the latex, and this mixture is poured

through a sieve to remove dirt, twigs, and bark.

A chemical called **formic acid**

is added to the latex.

This makes the latex thicken,

and solid pieces float to the surface.

These solid pieces of latex are called **crude rubber.**

Crude rubber is sent all over the world in huge ships. In the harbor, the bales of crude rubber are loaded onto trains, which take them to rubber factories.

In some rubber factories,
the crude rubber is cut into small pieces
by a machine with a huge knife.
It is then mixed with chemicals
that will make the rubber stronger and last longer.

A machine mixes the rubber with the chemicals.
Then the machine heats the rubber mixture
until a thick paste forms.

The rubber paste is poured into molds made of steel
and, with still more heat, is pressed into tires.
A special fabric is worked into the rubber
to make the tires strong and to keep them
from bursting.

Tires made from rubber are used on cars, buses, airplanes, bicycles, and other vehicles.
Many other products are made from rubber, too, such as rafts, soccer balls, balloons, rubber bands, and hoses.

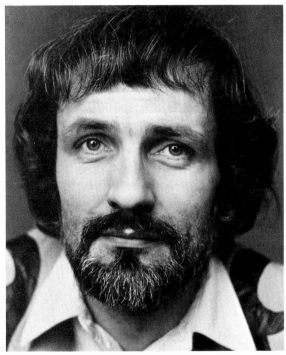

Ali
Mitgutsch

ALI MITGUTSCH is one of Germany's best-known children's book illustrators. He is a devoted world traveler, and many of his book ideas have taken shape during his travels. Perhaps this is why they have such international appeal. Mr. Mitgutsch's books have been published in 22 countries and are enjoyed by thousands of readers around the world.

Ali Mitgutsch lives with his wife and three children in Schwabing, the artists' quarter in Munich. The Mitgutsch family also enjoys spending time on their farm in the Bavarian countryside.

THE CAROLRHODA

START

TO FINISH
BOOKS